# THE TOMORROW BOOK OF VERSE

Poems by

## ELSBETH LIEBOWITZ

With illustrations by

### ROGER CURLEY

## OVERBOARD PRESS
### DENVER, COLORADO

First edition published in 1993 by

Overboard Press
5840 East Evans Avenue, Suite 201
Denver, Colorado 80222

ISBN 0-9636373-0-4

Manufactured in the United States of America

# CONTENTS

# THE TOMORROW BOOK OF VERSE

# INTRODUCTION

The planet, Mars, is a bone-rock red
without flowers, grass, or trees,
water, air, birds, or people, and
it's pocked like a red Swiss cheese.

Yet way off in the galaxy
are people-things who work and play,
chit-chat and go to school and bed
throughout their night and day.

Oh, they might look like sausages,
bananas bent to yellow hoops,
dill pickles spinning end over end,
or taffy pulled into loops.

They might be any shape or size
with ears and feet like custard pies.
So, what of that? Why must they be
like Eddy, Joe, Steve, or me?

Now nobody lives on Jupiter,
a monster world so far from the sun,
it's colder than ice and always night
where an ounce weighs like a ton.

Yet deep in the Dippers there are worlds
where people wonder: Could there be
anything in this Universe
a smidgen as smart as we?

They might look like ballooning lambs
fat elephants in rocking chairs,
flip-floppy, leaping lily pads,
or galloping Teddy bears.

They might be any size or shape
with bat wings of adhesive tape.
So, what of that? Why must they be
like Mom, Dad, Lynn, or me?

# TWELVE HANDS

If I had twelve hands instead of just two
you know what I'd do? You know what I'd do?

Some of those hands I'd use as a tail
to swing round and round, and whirl-away, sail!

Or I'd shovel up things to stash in my pockets
like airplanes, baboons, and electric eye sockets.

I'd reach up those hands to model a zoo
from thunderhead chimneys, a lolla-palloo.

Then I'd signal my pals way up in the stars
by strumming on quasar galactic guitars.

That's what I'd do, yes, that's what I'd do
if I had twelve hands, instead of just two.

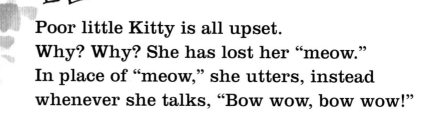

Poor little Kitty is all upset.
Why? Why? She has lost her "meow."
In place of "meow," she utters, instead
whenever she talks, "Bow wow, bow wow!"

Poor Freckles, the spaniel, is sad and upset.
Why? Why? He has lost his "bow wow."
In place of his bark, he mutters, instead,
"Moo moo moo," much like a cow.

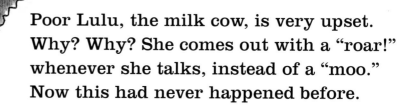

Poor Lulu, the milk cow, is very upset.
Why? Why? She comes out with a "roar!"
whenever she talks, instead of a "moo."
Now this had never happened before.

Huge Andy, the lion, is sputtering rage.
Why? Why? He gargles, somehow,
when he tries to talk, so in place of his "roar!"
out comes piping a tiny "meow!"

10

A head-scratching scientist rushes along
to see what in Nature's Laws could have gone wrong.
With bottles, burners, strange liquids and stuff
he concocts a magical poof! and a puff!

Away, away, all jumble, away!
The mixup is righted, and what's gone astray
is reshuffled in swish-swish and turned back around.
Once more, everyone makes his regular sound.

"Meow, meow!" sings Kitty, "Meow!"
while Freckles barks joyously, "Bow wow wow!"
"Moo, moo, moo," croons Lulu, the cow,
while ground and trees shuddering ten counties wide
proud Andy bellows, "REEOAOAOR, GRRROW!"
spearheading an endless, uproarious pride!

11

# DOODLESACK LANE

I went for a walk down Doodlesack Lane
while holding to my eyes
my little doll, Jane,
who swelled and swelled to such a size
her head rammed through the skies.

Oh, Jane, you're now so big
you could leap Meadow Falls in a jig!

Come, bend down, Jane, and lift me high
so I can poke and pat the sky!

Wow! Are those toys below that crawl?
No no, it's traffic shrunken small—
buses, autos, and trucks for my hand
with people tiny grains of sand,
and Winfield County's only a map
that's spread out low on my Jane's lap!

Oh Jane, you're now so great
you could cradle all New York State!

I then asked Jane, would she oblige
and hold me close up to her eyes
so I, in turn, could swell in size.

Oops! Jane, it is, who's shrinking small
until she's only inches tall
while I glide down to a swelling street
and once again I find my feet
walking as they'd been before
Jane had begun to soar.

Buses and autos are fuming by
with people normal grownup size.
How dim and high, a murky sky!

In ease, she drops, afloat—
Jane, softly as a mote.

While on a walk down Doodlesack Lane
I push in a pram my by-low, Jane,
once more her baby size,
not anywhere near my eyes!

# PERKLE STATE FAIR

Come, joggle with me in my Model-T flivver.
Four wheels it has as it shimmies and shivers,
black dust in the air to hide the back spare
while twentyone-hundred-three spectators stare
in my show at the Perkle State Fair.

Come, jiggle with me in my Model-J flivver.
Eight wheels it has, aquiver in shivers,
dust blotting out air to give you a scare
as twentyone-thousand-three spectators stare
in my show at the Perkle State Fair.

Come, zero! with me in my PDQ flivver.
*No* wheels it has as it gleams like a river
that spritzes through air with a flim and a flare
while zilliony-billions of spectators stare
in my show at the Perkle State Fair.

Come, vanish! with me in my Y-to-Z flivver,
streamlined like a dolphin, a shimmery quiver
that streaks, a blue trace, toward another *new* Space!
Hear those zilliony-trillions halloo in the glare!
So long, show, at the Perkle State Fair!

# FROM OTHER WORLDS

Oh, man, what a dream!
Who is this I see
from way off in Space
here visiting me?

With rainbowy scales
on six wavy tails,
through trumpets he talks
that he swivels on stalks.

Oh, are people from other worlds queer!
So different from what we are here.

Say, who can that be
with big Eddy, now,
from way off in Space?
An eagle? Or cow?

He's a four-headed duck
on a million-wheeled truck
kilometers high
quack-quacking the sky.

Though he's so unlike Eddy and me,
look! look! It's a *person*, we see!

Says a person way off
on the planet Laruss,
"What's this on another world
brewing a fuss?

"Just one knob for a head
and no wheels, but instead,
on two pins, there, he stands
waving two . . . *jointed wands?*

Is that oval he's kicking
with one of his pins
a smarter or dumber head
out for a spin?

See how the thing arcs
as lots of him tumble,
knobs every which-way
in—man! What a jumble!

Is it a message they're trying to send?
Or a civilization's end?

Oh, are creatures from other worlds queer!
So different from what we are here."

# DOUBLE-O-WORLD

Away way off in Space somewhere
is a world like ours, same water and air
and everyone here has a double out there—
Mom, Dad, and I—so we're all paired.

It's double-O you and a double-O me
on a double-O world in our galaxy.

My brother, Joe, and sister, Lynn,
Steve Fong and I, each has a twin
and when we work or fight or play
sleep at night or eat in the day
so do our doubles in the Milky Way.

It's double-O you and a double-O me
on a double-O world in our galaxy.

Joe, Steve and I are eating pie
and marshmallow whip with Lynn and Hy
while our twin world doubles are doing it, too,
out there in a stardust peekaboo.

And when we board a jet to go
to China, France, or Mexico,
so do our copies way out there
in the double-O world where we are paired.

Hello, me, in the galaxy!
Let's say we're friends with cake and tea.
Come, join us, Joe, Steve, Hy, and Lynn,
paired—each of us—with our otherworld twin!

It's double-O you and a double-O me,
double-O Joe, Lynn, Steve, and Lee,
away out in the galaxy.

Hey, Joe! It's getting late, you know.
There's a red, red glow, our sun is low,
and shadowy dew falls here and there
in the double-O world where we are paired.
So good night, doubles, 'til another fun day
for a whip-ding again in a double-O play!

19

# IF I COULD FLY

If I could fly just like a bird
where I would then make sure to go
is to the ranch of Cowboy Jim
to watch his mustang rodeo.

Now this is hot air in balloons, of course,
like flights to the moon on a rocking horse.
But maybe it can be done
if we set our antennae to "fun."

If I could fly just like a bird
I'd visit Greg, the talking frog,
where he and I could chat, then star
in his TV show on a quivery log.

Now really, nobody can do this,
since Greg needs his ventriloquist!
But maybe it can be done
if we set our dials to "fun."

If I could fly just like a bird
where I would then make sure to be
is on the spaceship Victory
that's making a tour of the galaxy.

You're kidding, it's people who work and try,
not sensible birds, to get up *that* high!
So, sense be blown in a breeze,
while people jump planets with ease.

# MULLAMAGEE

On the far planet of Mullamagee
money is funny and everything's free,
with shopping centers among the trees.

Money grows in the shrubbery
as apples, cherries,
and honey dew blossoms,
while checkout people
are deer and opossums.
Monkeys cavort
around checkout stands
where we chatter and somersault—
then we shake hands.

Now we float down the mall
with our shopping carts
which, from a pink sky,
receive lollipop tarts
with puppies and kittens
to cuddle our hearts.

Then the sky shimmers sauce
on scoops of ice cream
that meld with orange
and lemonade streams
topped with sugar-plum money
as Weekends supreme.

What a delicious money-dew Sunday
for our delight in a year-long fun-day!

On the far planet of Mullamagee
yes, marketing's different
where money floats free.

# GABBLEDEGANNET

Where sea lions curl their whiskers with spoons
and elephants ride pink balloons
while dining on green macaroons
and bullfrogs ride hippopotami
that tightrope on laser beams up to ten moons
to the ruffle of ruckety drums
and toucans' yakety tunes,
yes, this is the planet
of Gabbledegannet.

Where humans are animals in the zoo
in cages of toffee and glue
and their keepers are rhesus and gnu
who nibble the bars for gumchungery snacks
while scratching each others' backs,
where elephants, eland, and grizzly bears
gape and throw peanuts and prickly pears
at humans in cages upended in air,
yes, this is the planet
of Gabbledegannet.

People or animals, who is who,
depends on who owns the planet and zoo,
who slings the peanuts and prickly pears
and who are the caged upending in air,
flumpery trumpeting, scream, roar or moo,
as they vie for the missiles that globber in goo.

Rickety rackety, Gabbledegannet—
why, I'd as soon stay
right here on *my* planet!

# FUN SPACE FLIGHT

When the astronauts fly to the moon
in a module packed like a cocoon,
they're bundled up fast,
tumbling each in a cast,
for they cannot walk free
nor breathe nor talk free
'til they're safe back on Earth through a blast.

But Eddy, Joe, Steven, and I,
high-jumping, can vault the whole sky
as though we're balloons
on a hot afternoon,
while Outer Space swings, rockabye.

Then, each on an air-pocket sleigh,
we're lickety! light-years away,
tobogganing, zoom!
along meteor plumes
in the span of a googleplex day.

So we zip, whirl-a-whizz!
spinning networks of fizz
while churning up meteor showers.

What a fun world, so different from ours!
Where gravity springs as you please
with spaceships from holes in Swiss cheese.

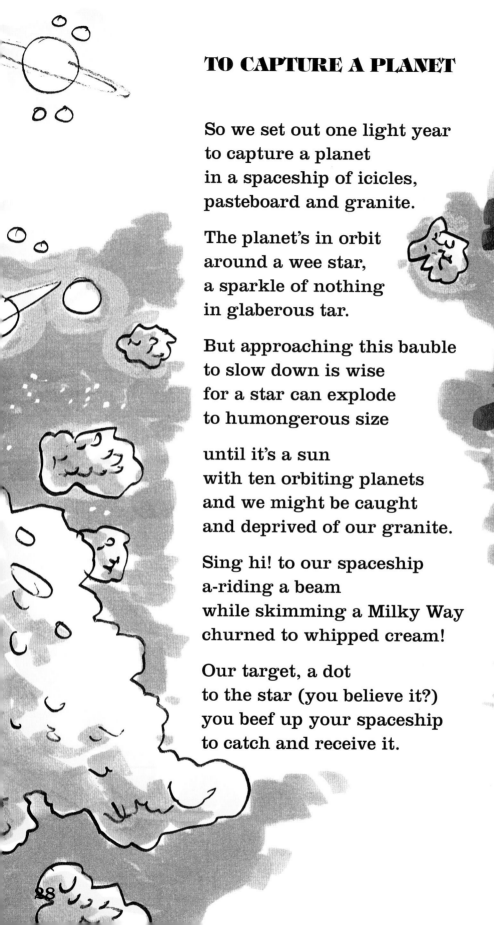

# TO CAPTURE A PLANET

So we set out one light year
to capture a planet
in a spaceship of icicles,
pasteboard and granite.

The planet's in orbit
around a wee star,
a sparkle of nothing
in glaberous tar.

But approaching this bauble
to slow down is wise
for a star can explode
to humongerous size

until it's a sun
with ten orbiting planets
and we might be caught
and deprived of our granite.

Sing hi! to our spaceship
a-riding a beam
while skimming a Milky Way
churned to whipped cream!

Our target, a dot
to the star (you believe it?)
you beef up your spaceship
to catch and receive it.

Next battle that furnace
with volleys of quarks
fired from popguns
on space Noah's arks.

Our choice is a gem
made of grapefruit, blue plum,
red cherries, bananas,
and honeydew rum.

When we've conquered the mon-star
we'll tow the gem home
and store it forever
under the Capitol Dome.

# TUMBLING UPWARDS

We shuck off our gravity,
bid it goodbye,
then boarding an air pocket
zip! to the sky.

One, two, we break through
the upper air blue
to rush into blackness
a-loop, and halloo!

Oh, look through the stars
way out in pitch dark
are planets like ours
among drizzles of sparks!

Hello, there, you people!
We're streaking along
to meet you and play with you
signalling song!

Now some of you folks
look like eagles and loons
while others shape up
as giraffes and baboons.

Gazelles leap ballets
on Saturn's rings
while wallabies lollop
in space-way flings.

To the left, ship ahoy!
I see Mother and Dad
about to take off
from a gingerbread pad.

To the right a pink lion
roves planet Gallee
with Norry, a green boy
who's waving at me.

He looks something like me
except he is green
wearing nothing at all
while I must wear jeans.

Come aromas of dinner
we signal goodbye,
reharnessed in gravity,
dining on sundae-moon pie.

# JEDDLE-DEE-JOOP

Through our radar echo balloon
Jeddle-Dee-Joop, you and I are in tune.
Although you are so enormously far
that in between us float shivers of stars
and though you're built so differently
from people here, including me,
we're both children who hate
to go to bed other than very late.

Do you get spanked by lashing flippers?
Or, my star friend, are those fins
that serve as whippers?
How I try to understand
the movement of your feet, your hands,
your head, and how you eat!

What? You have no hands or feet?

Does your head swivel back and forth
on some hidden stump or stalk
between . . . those are your shoulders
hunched up like two fuzzy boulders?
How you glide, instead of walk!
What is your body? Jointed eggs?
And are those flippers, arms, or legs?

Oh, Jeddle-Dee-Joop in an orbiting loop
a million light years away,
what fun if my backyard could extend
to yours, and we would be friends
in identical days at play!

But different as our worlds may be,
you, in tomorrow or yesterday
(how like a cherry is your sun!),
fooling and pranks are so much fun
we do agree
despite your queer anatomy.

And so, out there, let's keep in tune
like song through our radar balloon
and let's not ever forget
there was a time we almost met
though in between us, you and me,
rides most of our great galaxy!

# TIM TOM CAT

I have a friend from the planet M'daws,
a virtuoso with ten paws.

With a himmel-lee booma-lee
Do re mi
old Tim Tom Cat
plays the rheostat
plicka-pat-a-pat timpany.

He travels on a laser beam through space
flipping dadderoos as a tumbling ace.

A master of the rheostat
he looks much like a ten-legged cat.

With a himmel-lee, booma-lee
Do re mi
old Tim Tom Cat
plays the rheostat
Plicka-pit-a-pat timpany.

From dolla-whipped clouds he churns up zoos
with yellow catamounts, pink cockatoos,

blue elephants, buff stegosaurs,
and broncos charging over yucca-tan shores.

With a himmel-lo tremolo
la ti do
old Tim Tom Cat
on the rheostat
corrals a rodeo.

He plays rainbows on his rheostat
through radar whiskers, plicka-tat-tat.

He's a buckaroo who rides the keys
in stella-rado roundup harmonies.

With a himmel-lo tremolo
la ti do
old Tim Tom Cat
on the rheostat
corrals a rodeo.

Old Tim Tom Cat pays me a call,
strumming on a rope the Gimme Caterwaul.

Then buckaroos kick up their heels
along relays in planetary reels

while dogies prance around a ring
of starlight mist to the rope's gay *ping!*

Then a yippy hi yay! And a laser track
set Tom toward M'daws for the trip on back.

With a himmel-lo tremolo
la ti do
old Tim Tom Cat
on the rheostat
corrals a rodeo.

Stick horses dance the bronco buck
as Tim Tom plays, "So long, good luck!"

With a himmel-lo tremolo
la ti do
old Tim Tom Cat
from his rheostat
turns off the rodeo.

# EXPLORING WORLDS

We've got a spaceship asteroid
designed by Eddy, built by Floyd,
and why we're voyaging through space is
to pay calls on other races
way out in the void.
Earth, here, has become such a bore
that we can't take it anymore.
Now listen to the countdown, ticking, so,
to zero. Wham! And here we go!

Hello, out there, hello!
We're right on target whizzing through
the starry nothing, straight to you,
and here we are, yoohoo!

Our first stop is a world of dogs
who greet us in a mass
of switching tails and barks and yaps
through tall and crackly grass.

They're friendly, oh, but what a racket
as they lick our knees
then jump on us, crawl under us,
and oops! have they got fleas!

Scratch scratch, and ow! We hurry, but fast,
back to our asteroid!
From bites and yaps, we sprint on board
then zero for the void.

Hello, out there, we're coming,
we're whizzing through to you
across a starry stretch of nothing.
Here we are, yoohoo!

Our next world is a steamy one
of monster dinosaurs.
As high as trees, they gather toward us
more and more and more.

It's sticky hot, we start to sweat,
as one tyrannosaur
glares down at us with others, too,
who now begin to roar!

Oh, man, we'd better leave, skiddoo!
For all those beady eyes
give us a clue, they think we're dinner.
We think otherwise.

It's back back to our asteroid
but fast! We sprint on board.
At once, we're streaking toward the void.
Goodbye, you dinosaurs!

Hello, out there, we're coming,
we're zooming! through to you
straight toward the brightest part of nothing.
Here we are, yoohoo!

Where we are now is civilized,
a world of elephants
who, though gigantic, waltz around us
in a stately dance.

They bow their heads and raise their trunks
and one says, "Who are you?
A bunch of apes we'd better take
right to our *human* zoo!"

With trunks up high, they try to catch us
fiercely convinced that we
are animals they ought to cage.
How we fight to break free!

At last, at last, our crew escapes
to beeline for the ship.
We're just in time, we close the hatches
with a zap! and a zip!

Hello, hello, we're coming,
we're whizzing through to you
straight back to where the black is blackest.
Here we are, yoohoo!

We next call on a world of monkeys,
yellow, brown, and pink.
All gussied up like grinder's monkeys,
how they prank and prink!

They have no tails, they have no fleas,
and they don't try to eat us,
nor try to cage us for their zoos.
In fact, some flock to greet us.

But oh! the racket that they make!
They're worse than dogs for noise!
So filthy dirty is their world
it shocks us, girls and boys!

Perhaps we ought to cage this monkeys,
put them in a zoo,
then tidy up their messy world
to make it good as new.

We set to work, we like this world,
and think of staying here.
But oh! these monkeys are so pesky,
how they interfere!

We try to scrub and scrape and scrunge
for all this planet's worth.
Our asteroid is in its berth.
Hey, Floyd—we're back on earth!

# THE GRANDEST RIDE

Danny went for a walk in the park,
inventing a pet on the way.
A cloud in the air kept changing its shape
to a gnu, then a hippo at bay.

"I want an elephant!" Danny exclaimed.
The pet began to obey.
"No, no!" Danny piped. "It's a puppy I want!"
And the cloud was a puppy at play.

"Oh, how do you do it, Danny?" asked Bill.
Janet was wondering, too.
Said Danny, "My pet will do what I want,
like becoming a gullamaroo.

Just look at that eagle-winged kangaroo
up there! Oh, now it's a bear."
Then Danny whistled up to his pet
that whoosh! dropped down through the air.

Mounting the bear, now a dinosaur,
Danny whistled again.
Then up, up they rose to a hill in the sky.
Zing! to the count of ten.

"Well, how about that?" said Janet to Linda
as Michael and Jerry strolled by.
"If Danny can get himself up to the sky
why can't we all? Let's try!"

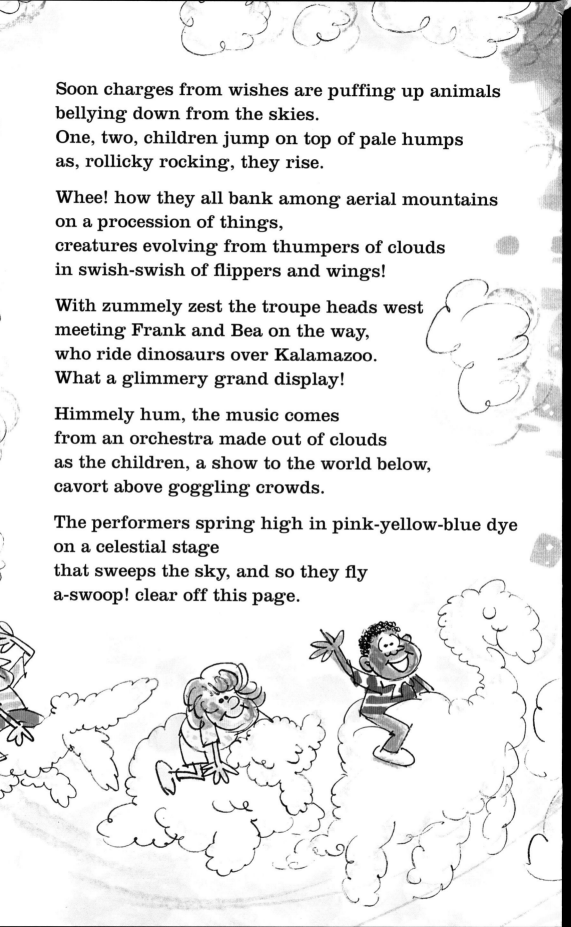

Soon charges from wishes are puffing up animals
bellying down from the skies.
One, two, children jump on top of pale humps
as, rollicky rocking, they rise.

Whee! how they all bank among aerial mountains
on a procession of things,
creatures evolving from thumpers of clouds
in swish-swish of flippers and wings!

With zummely zest the troupe heads west
meeting Frank and Bea on the way,
who ride dinosaurs over Kalamazoo.
What a glimmery grand display!

Himmely hum, the music comes
from an orchestra made out of clouds
as the children, a show to the world below,
cavort above goggling crowds.

The performers spring high in pink-yellow-blue dye
on a celestial stage
that sweeps the sky, and so they fly
a-swoop! clear off this page.

# NEVER-SUCH-THING

One morning sweet Never-Such-Thing flickered by
and together in spirals we winked to the sky.
Rainbows began to xylophone songs
where puppies and pandas billowed in throngs
and elephants, trunking, fanned wide their ears
to welcome as passengers monkeys and deer.

A mockingbird chorus kept caroling strong:
oh, it's through you that northern lights sing
where people ride tremolos, Never-Such-Thing,
and far planets woo us to which we can fly
and feast on pear sundae and honeydew pie,
where dolphins and walruses often discuss
physics and logic while cuddling ducks,
and cattle and sheep who chortle delight
wherever giraffes lope, flying their kites.

Now lickety-rocking I turn in my chair
on a rosy rhinoceros sailing blue air
while centered above us on rainbows in pairs
as on two circus horses stands Never-Such-Thing,
and crowding below her, we friends in the blue
mounted on hippos, red-tailed kangaroo,
ostriches, camels, an aerial zoo,
with flippers, hump-dingers, and undulant wings,
laugh as we pierce silky blue into black
where Milky Way dolphins are blazing a track.

Then up, up we fall into silvery shawls
where unicorns caper and zebras abound.
Ding! off her rainbows leaps Never-Such-Thing
to play golden scales on crocodile tails
'til suns with their jingly planets resound
making the galaxy ring.

Zip! we ride rapids in lemonade foam,
when blip! here's bed, and home. . . .

# GREEN BOY

One hot and muggy day in June
Eddy, Steve, and I
are looking upward at the sky
where clouds are whisking by.

The sky is golden, orange and blue.
Eddy is chocolate brown,
Steven is yellow, I am pink—
when a green cloud dips down.

The cloud is shaped like a giant boy
we earth boys think we see
when suddenly it whooshes closer,
shrinking rapidly

until it stands among us three
of boy-size, very green,
the strangest color for a person
we have ever seen,

with diamond eyes and green hair misting
'round an emerald face,
for Norry is a green boy,
a visitor from outer space.

At once we're way up in the sky
floating with gulls and hawks.
No flight nor climb, we're just up there
on airy rides and walks.

Fresh winds are blowing all about
as in delicious scare
we flip, yahoo! where up and down
are both made out of air!

Suddenly, ballooning pink,
a country's swinging by
with poodles, potatoes, porpoises,
and cream puffs dolloping high.

One, two, we're floating up whipped cream
when charging at a slant
through fleecy layers, with ears like fans,
looms Al, the elephant.

He's orange and rose and rears a trunk
that trumpets shimmery light.
"Hi! Welcome, Norry! Good to see you!
Come, let's tour the sights!

"But these three lumps that mimic you,
what are they doing here?
They have no sheen, they flop and flump.
Ugh! How their outlines smear!

"They'd better be siphoned back to earth
before they dissipate
and pop their filth and nastiness
throughout our sky estate!"

"Oh, no!" cry Eddy, Steve, and I.
"Don't make us go back down!
We promise we'll take lots of baths!"
But big Al rumbles, frowns.

Then Norry pleads, "Al, these are my friends.
I know they aren't strong
or smart, but I'll look after them.
Please let them tag along."

"Well, all right," thunders Al in flashes.
"But they must not fall
or fuss, drip dirt, disintegrate,
or bother me at all!"

He hunkers down, big columns kneel,
we small-fry flip on board,
four boys through a charge from Norry—
when Zarroom! we soar!

Somehow, Al's columns straighten long.
Zip! we streak up a flue,
a nimbus chimney-elevator,
up to what a view!

To a piping laser *tom too tee!*
we're lifted off Al's back,
drawn by Norry's electronics
on to a feathery track.

The sky is washed in crystal sunshine.
Without gravity
rounding tops of giant oranges
we float high and free!

Ow! Ow! I'm tripping on an anvil!
Help! I'm starting to fall!
Eddy and Steve are following me
carom! in somersault!

Down down down swish! we pinwheel crazy
when, kerchunk! we stop.
Through clammy paste we're being hoisted
upward, toward the top.

Norry is peering down on us
from a bank of cloud.
"I told you so, I told you so!"
Al thunders, black and loud.

"Oh, Al!" pleads Norry, "I'm so sorry!
I can't figure why
my three friends keep on plummeting
and can't stay in the sky!

Please let them first take one last swim
before I blip them down.
They're so much fun and shaped like me.
(Oh, why don't they catch on?)"

I hope big Al will change his mind
and, though we flop and smear,
some day when we sharpen up,
he'll say, "Come join us here!"

# SPACE FREEWAY

There is a freeway through the sky
where folks ride spaceship cars
heading one way toward Mercury,
the other way skirting stars.

So, here's our car—Bill, Norry, Steve, Linda—
and yours—Eddy, Sue, Joe,
and Jane. Come, all of you, flip on board!
Three, two, one . . . here we go!

With green boy, Norry, at the helm,
we earthlings in our seats,
our heads are high to view the launch,
tucked near the floor, our feet—

when Eddy and Jane slue upside down.
No way can they see out.
"Hey, what's going on here?" Norry cries
as he whips round about.

"I've lost my bearings!" Eddy whimpers.
"Gosh, where are my feet?"
Then Norry winks a laser-flash.
Psst! Eddy's back in his seat.

Another flash, Jane's sitting, too,
where she had been before
with everyone now right-side up,
feet swinging near the floor.

On, on we voyage when we see
a wheeling Milky Way
where whales and dolphins, vaulting rainbows,
nuzzle and croon in play.

Up, up they zoom, and down they swoop
from mound to resonant mound
inviting us to join them in
their concertizing rounds.

"Oh, let's go out and swim with them!"
Linda and Steven cry.
"Just what are those big white balls?" Joe adds.
"They look like icecream pie!"

"Those balls," says Norry, "are white flares
deep in the Milky Way,
not food. We cannot leave the ship
nor go outside to play—

"so just calm down, set back your seats
until this car alights.
Not one of you could breathe out there!
Relax! Enjoy the sights!"

"I'm getting hungry," Bobby whines.
"Oh, when're we going to eat?"
When Norry on a starry organ
pipes to a strumalo beat:

"Ready and calm for dinner-time,
Zip! through an ampersand
at a buffet banquet ten miles long,
we're zeroing in to land!"

# AUTHOR'S NOTE

Elsbeth Liebowitz was born in New York City in 1918 and graduated from Washburn University in Topeka, Kansas, in the 1950s. A self-described "late bloomer," she has worked slowly for several decades to develop the unique mixture of imagination and original thinking that characterizes *The Tomorrow Book of Verse*. "In my opinion," she writes, "fantasy has been short-changed in children's literature today. I hope young readers will discover in my book the kind of imaginative energy that stimulates their own flights of fancy." Ms. Liebowitz is currently at work on a book of poetry for adults.

# ILLUSTRATOR'S NOTE

Roger Curley has been a professional illustrator for 25 years and currently creates his art in Dublin, Ohio. About his work in *The Tomorrow Book of Verse,* he has written: "Elsbeth Liebowitz has the ability to reach out beyond our everyday world and extract for our enjoyment bits and pieces of future fantasy. Thanks, Elsbeth! See you on Mullamagee!"